MY STORY TIME.

IS IT POSSIBLE?

TELMA GUIMARÃES

Illustrated by Enrico Marchi

Editora Saraiva

AN **ANT** IN AN **AIRPLANE** ?

A **BEAR** ON THE **BEACH** ?

A **CAMEL** IN A **COAT** ?

A **DUCK** IN THE **DESERT**?

AN **EAGLE** IN AN **EGG**?

A **FLEA** IN **FLUFF** ?

A **GIRL-GOAT**?

A **HEN** ON A **HILL**?

AN **ILL IBIS** ?

A **JOEY** IN THE **JUNGLE** ?

A **KITTY** IN THE **KITCHEN** ?

A **LION** IN THE **LIVING-ROOM** ?

A **MONKEY** IN THE **MALL** ?

A **NANNY-GOAT** IN A **NEST** ?

AN **OCTOPUS** IN AN **OPERA**?

A **PORCUPINE** IN A **POCKET** ?

A **QUAIL** IN A **QUILT** ?

A **RABBIT** IN A **RACE** ?

A **SNAKE** IN **SHOES** ?

A **TIGER** ON A **TRAIN**?

A **UNICORN** WITH AN **UMBRELLA** ?

A **VULTURE** ON A **VISIT** ?

A **WHALE** IN A **WINDOW** ?

A **X-MAS PARTY**
WITH ALL THE **FAMILY** ?

A **YELLOW BIRD** IN A **YARD**?

A **ZEBRA** WITH **ZIGZAG LINES** ?

THE AUTHOR

My name is Telma Guimarães. I was born in Marília, São Paulo. When I was a teenager, I took an Exchange program in Covington, Georgia. It was a wonderful experience. I graduated with a bachelor degree in Languages, English and Literature at UNESP. I moved to Campinas and then I started teaching English. I have three children and I loved telling stories to my kids. Many of the stories were created by me.

My heart was always full of joy when I sat on my chair and thought about children, animals, nature and so on. So, I gave up teaching and tried to reach my goal: to be an author. Here I am.

Quadro Europeu Comum de Referência para Línguas (CEFR)

A1 A2 B1 B2 C1 C2

Is it possible?

Presidência Mario Ghio Júnior

Vice-presidência de educação digital Camila Montero Vaz Cardoso

Direção editorial Lidiane Vivaldini Olo

Gerência editorial Julio Cesar Augustus de Paula Santos

Coordenação editorial Laura Vecchioli do Prado

Aprendizagem digital Renata Galdino (ger.), Beatriz de Almeida Pinto Rodrigues da Costa (coord. Experiência de Aprendizagem), Carla Isabel Ferreira Reis (coord. Produção Multimídia), Daniella dos Santos Di Nubila (coord. Produção Digital), Rogerio Fabio Alves (coord. Publicação), Vanessa Tavares Menezes de Souza (coord. Design Digital)

Planejamento, controle de produção e indicadores Flávio Matuguma (ger.), Juliana Batista (coord.) e Jayne Ruas (analista)

Edição Instituto Parole

Revisão Ray Shoulder e Maria Claudia Franchi

Ilustração, projeto gráfico e diagramação Enrico Esposito Marchi

Capa Thatiana Kalaes

Dados Internacionais de Catalogação na Publicação (CIP)

Guimarães, Telma
Is it possible? / Telma Guimarães ; ilustrações de Enrico Marchi.
-- 1. ed. – São Paulo : Saraiva, 2022.

ISBN 978-65-5867-111-4

1. Literatura infantojuvenil I. Título II. Marchi, Enrico

22-3786 CDD 028.5

Angélica Ilacqua - Bibliotecária - CRB-8/7057

CL: 531268

CAE: 795106

2022

1ª edição

1ª tiragem

Impressão e acabamento: Bartira

Saraiva

Direitos desta edição cedidos à Somos Sistemas de Ensino S.A.

Av. Paulista, 901, Bela Vista – São Paulo – SP – CEP 01310-200

Tel.: (0xx11) 4003-3061

Conheça o nosso portal de literatura Coletivo Leitor: www.coletivoleitor.com.br

Este livro foi composto nas fontes *Grenadine MVB* e
Prenton e impresso sobre papel off set 90 g/m2.